BRITAIN IN OLD PHOTOGRAPHS

UXBRIDGE, HILLINGDON & COWLEY

K . R .   P E A R C E

ALAN SUTTON PUBLISHING LIMITED

Alan Sutton Publishing Limited
Phoenix Mill · Far Thrupp · Stroud
Gloucestershire · GL5 2BU

First published 1995

Copyright © K.R. Pearce, 1995

Cover photographs: *(front) John Ward,*
carpenter and builder, with his workmen, in
Wellington Road, c. 1902; (back) Lord and
Lady Hillingdon in the grounds of Hillingdon
Court, c. 1918.

British Library Cataloguing in Publication Data.
A catalogue record for this book is available from
the British Library.

ISBN 0-7509-1037-2

Typeset in 9/10 Sabon.
Typesetting and origination by
Alan Sutton Publishing Limited.
Printed in Great Britain by
Hartnolls, Bodmin, Cornwall.

Contents

The western end of High Street, *c*. 1900. As yet there is no proper surface on the roadway. In the distance is the hump of the canal bridge, with the sign of the Swan and Bottle just above it. The building with white walls beyond the tree is the Crown and Treaty public house.

Introduction

This volume covers what is today the central area of the London Borough of Hillingdon – the ancient market town of Uxbridge, and the neighbouring former villages of Hillingdon and Cowley. After a brief historical introduction, the account carries the story of that district from late Victorian times through to the outbreak of the Second World War. It reveals how a primarily rural area of west Middlesex, based for centuries on farming, market-gardening and flour-milling, became affected by the westward sprawl of London in the early twentieth century. By 1907 the relatively small town of Uxbridge had three railway lines and a tram route – all of them termini! Thereafter the farms, fields, trees and hedgerows gave way to bricks, mortar, concrete and tarmac, although vestiges of the once rural community remained. The old photographs in this book enable the reader to look back at the area as it was over a century ago, and glimpse the rustic tranquillity and charm of that era. The reader is then conducted through the first four decades of the twentieth century, witnessing the development of road and rail transport, the move to light industry, the use of increased leisure time, the arrival of the Royal Air Force, and the changes in education and social habits. The book concludes with a look at a few notable personalities.

Lord Hillingdon's car with his chauffeur, William Maynard, at the wheel, *c.* 1918.

Looking towards the market house, High Street, *c.* 1900. Most of the shops are still in private hands, with the owner and his family living over the shop, but the presence of the Freeman, Hardy & Willis shoe shop on the extreme left is a reminder that the chain stores were beginning to appear.

THE HISTORICAL BACKGROUND

The market house and St Margaret's Church, c. 1910. Two historic buildings share a crowded site.

The market house from an early nineteenth-century print. The building dates from 1789, cost about £3,000, and must have been the biggest building in the town at the time. Plain and functional, it was once described as 'the bulbous nose of Uxbridge'. From about 1780 to 1840 the market house was the scene of one of the largest corn markets in the south of England.

The eastern end of the market house, c. 1900. The ground floor of the building was completely open to the weather at this time, hence the tarpaulins to protect the stallholders. Here stood an earlier market house, in existence by 1561. It was a square, two-storey building, but alas no drawing of it survives.

The western end of Uxbridge, drawn in 1818. In the foreground the river Colne flows under High Bridge. Beyond it is the canal bridge and the High Street. On the left is the Swan and Bottle public house. On the right is the Crown Inn (later the Crown and Treaty).

The Crown and Treaty public house, early twentieth century. The building is the west wing of what was once a large private house called The Place. Here, in 1645, Royalists and Parliamentarians met in an attempt to bring the Civil War to a close. For three weeks the talks continued, but no agreement was reached. Nevertheless people still call it The Treaty House.

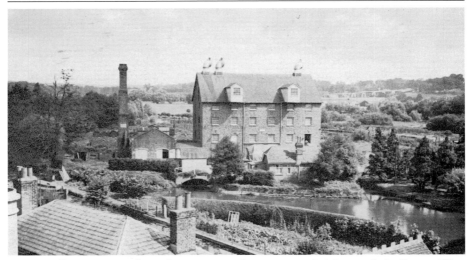

King's Mill, *c*. 1945. A flourishing corn market meant a thriving trade in flour milling on the rivers Colne and Fray's. In the early nineteenth century there were said to be ten mills in the neighbourhood of Uxbridge. Of those only one, King's Mill, survives as a working mill. In about 1530 a landowner named John Fray had diverted water from the river Colne to increase the flow of water in an existing tributary. This became known as Fray's river, and eventually powered five flour mills.

The western end of Uxbridge, *c*. 1900. In the foreground is the Swan and Bottle public house and the river Colne with High Bridge. Fray's river is visible in the distance. Between the two runs the Grand Junction Canal with industrial development visible on its banks, particularly the Osborne, Stevens timber yard.

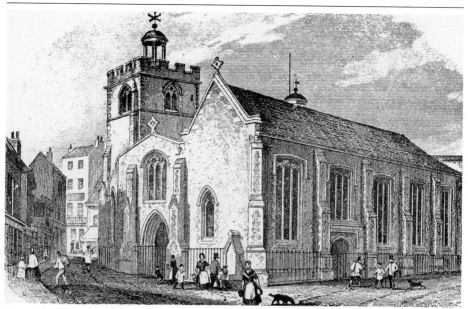

St Margaret's Church from a Victorian print. It is a view instantly recognisable today. What makes the church unusual is that there is no churchyard. For centuries St Margaret's was a chapel-of-ease of Hillingdon and burials took place there. The town acquired its own burial ground in 1576, and parish status as late as 1827.

The Militia Barracks, Villier Street. This headquarters was built for the Royal Elthorne Light Infantry Militia in 1855. This project, together with the coming of the Great Western Railway in 1856, led to the development of south Uxbridge and the Greenway area.

St Andrew's Church, *c.* 1910. The increase in population in south Uxbridge led to the need for a new parish, and, in 1856, the parish of St Andrew, Hillingdon West came into being. Its church, designed by Sir George Gilbert Scott, has a fine spire which dominated the district.

Colham Green, early twentieth century. To the south of Hillingdon lay the hamlet of Colham, of relatively minor importance. It is sobering to realise that, in 1086, the manor of Colham formed the greater part of the district; within it lay a small settlement called Wxebruge. There were smaller manors at Hillingdon and Cowley.

LATE VICTORIAN
TIMES

*Uxbridge Football Club in the 1870s. Founded in 1871, the club had a Maltese cross as
its emblem in the early years. Their home ground was Uxbridge Common.*

High Street, *c.* 1870. The view is from the market house looking towards the St Andrew's end. The tall building on the right now houses branches of the Halifax Building Society and the Midland Bank; just beyond it the sign of the Three Tuns overhangs the pavement. Plate glass windows were things of the future.

Vine Street, *c.* 1905. On the right is the GWR station, the terminus of a branch line from the main route at West Drayton, opened in 1856. The tall shop in the distance, on the right, is Randall's stores, founded there in 1891.

Rabbs Mill, *c.* 1890. A flour mill on the Fray's river, it stood at the junction of Cowley Road and Cowley Mill Road, and was known, at other times, as Austin's Mill and Dobell's Mill (see page 17). Near here today stands a thirteen-storey tower block named Rabbs Mill House.

Hay-making, Hundred Acres, 1900. Mrs Jones, complete with bonnet and dress with leg-o-mutton sleeves, rakes the hay together. Her husband, William, and his brother, Harry, fork it on to a cart pulled by a bullock. Today the factory of Arthur Sanderson and Sons occupies this site.

Cherry-picking, Cowley House orchard. To the south of Uxbridge lay much flat, fertile soil with orchards and market gardens. Using these enormous ladders with splayed bases, the men filled baskets with fruit. A man with a shotgun scares the birds away.

Uxbridge Volunteer Fire Brigade, *c.* 1895. The brigade was established in 1865, with headquarters in Windsor Street. The horse-drawn Merryweather appliance shown here was bought by public subscription in 1881, and christened 'Perseverance'.

Rabbs Mill, 1898. Fire broke out on Sunday 10 February and the blaze was so fierce that the mill was completely destroyed. Here the workforce assist the Fire Brigade in clearing the charred debris. The mill was later rebuilt (see page 58).

Belmont, near Uxbridge Common. Built in about 1810, it replaced an earlier house of the same name which had been erected in around 1700. The Belmont estate occupied much of the area which is now North Uxbridge. The house was demolished in 1931 and Belmont Close occupies the site today.

The Wakefield family, Belmont, 1886. Charles Wakefield (1838–1902), wearing the bowler hat, came from a family with business interests in Birmingham and New Zealand. He acquired the house in about 1877. His wife Annette, in the floral hat, was an active supporter of local schools and charities. Note the toy horse on wheels and the goat-cart for the children.

Uxbridge Cottage Hospital, Park Road. It was established in 1868, largely owing to the efforts of the Cox family who then owned Hillingdon House (now RAF Uxbridge). Maintained by public subscription, it had five single-bed wards on the first floor. It closed in 1914, when a larger building opened in Harefield Road.

Hillingdon Workhouse and chapel. Opened in 1747, the original building was enlarged in 1837 when it became the workhouse for Uxbridge, Ruislip, Norwood, West Drayton and Harmondsworth. The chapel was added in 1875. At the end of the last century there were about 250 inmates. In more recent times the workhouse has been transformed into Hillingdon Hospital.

Prince Albert Lodge Oddfellows with their banner, 1887. They are almost certainly celebrating Queen Victoria's Golden Jubilee. There were five such societies in Uxbridge at the time, offering men social activities and a sickness benefit scheme. In 1893 the local Oddfellows had a membership of 500.

The Uxbridge Volunteers, Harlington, c. 1886. They are on their way to attend a battalion parade at Hounslow. Their full title was E (Uxbridge) Company, 2nd Volunteer Battalion, Duke of Cambridge's Own Middlesex Regiment. In 1907 these volunteer forces became Territorial Battalions.

Junction of Park Road and High Street, *c.* 1900. A council cart is engaged on snow-clearing work. The Uxbridge Urban District Council came into being in 1895. At this period severe weather occurred almost every winter, and skating on local rivers, canals and lakes took place regularly.

High Street, Uxbridge, 1897. Tradesmen's vans parade during the Diamond Jubilee celebrations. The competition for the best turned-out van was judged in the grounds of Hillingdon House, and the vehicles then toured the town.

Members of Old Meeting Congregational church, 1897. They are enjoying their summer outing at Warren Farm, Harefield Road. A companion photograph showing all the children exists, but unfortunately is badly damaged. The bearded man seated on the extreme left is the Minister, Revd Robert Sewell. Hats were in vogue! Old Meeting was the oldest Nonconformist church in Uxbridge with a history dating back to 1662. The building is now known as Watts Hall, and forms part of the Christ Church premises.

Mixed class, St Andrew's School, *c.* 1890. The opening of St Andrew's Church in 1865 soon led to a demand for a parish school. St Andrew's School was established in January 1869, as a girls' and infants' school.

Miss Thonger's school, Montague Road, *c.* 1895. This dame school was run by Emma Thonger, who came from a family of saddlers and harness makers. On the extreme right is Dorothy Grey, whose father manufactured lemonade and ginger beer at premises in Vine Street.

Uxbridge FC, the old Crystal Palace ground, 23 April 1898. 'The Reds' had reached the final of the FA Amateur Cup, and were about to take the field against Middlesbrough FC. Middlesbrough won 2–0, and promptly turned professional. The players are, back row, left to right: E. Benstead, H. Skinner, G. Gumbrell, F. Brown, H. Gayland, A. Jacobs. Seated: A.R. Woodbridge, W. Hickman, E. Browning, W.J. Knight, E.W. Woodbridge.

Uxbridge Caxtonian FC, *c.* 1886. Another local side, this was composed, as their name suggests, of workers in the print trade. They took part in the West Middlesex Cup competition in the 1885–6 season. The earliest mention of the game in this district was at Ruislip in 1576, when seven Uxbridge men were involved in 'football, by reason of which unlawful game there rose amongst them a great affray, likely to result in homicides and serious accidents' (Middlesex Sessions records).

Cycling club, Uxbridge Metropolitan Police, Windsor Street police station, 1900. By this time cycling had become a very popular hobby and Londoners were beginning to come out into the countryside of West Middlesex and South Buckinghamshire at weekends and bank holidays.

Road menders, Colham Green, c. 1900. Cycling may have been popular, but at times it was not a particularly comfortable sport. Many roads were full of pot holes and ridges, especially in winter. These men are using picks to loosen and level the surface.

These two views come from *Album of Uxbridge and Neighbourhood*. It appeared in 1898, and was doubtless aimed at the 'tourists' on their cycling trips. The top picture shows Uxbridge town centre, with the market house on the left. The buildings on the right include three public houses: the Ram, the Bell and the Sun. The lower photograph shows the St Andrew's end of the High Street, with the market house turret just visible in the distance. On the left are large private houses; on the right trees of the Park Lodge estate. Note the mounted policeman.

Section Three

COWLEY IN
ABOUT 1900

The northern end of Cowley High Street, looking towards Uxbridge, c. 1905.

St Laurence's Church, *c.* 1900. It is the smallest medieval church in Middlesex. Dating from the twelfth century, it replaced an earlier building belonging to the monks of Westminster Abbey. The west porch, bell turret and spire were added in 1780. The area of grass in the foreground was consecrated as an extension to the churchyard in 1903. The almshouses on the left were built for the poor of the parish in 1776, but were demolished in 1950. That site also became part of the churchyard.

Cowley Church of England School, High Street. On the left is the schoolteacher's house. The school was constructed in 1891 to replace the one built near the parish church in 1836. Extensions were added on the north side in 1933–4; the school moved to a new site in Worcester Road in the 1950s.

The Crown Inn, High Street, *c.* 1900. The gate on the right advertises 'Good Stabling'. Although the inn was supplied at this time by Ashby's Brewery, it later came under the control of the Uxbridge-based Harman's Brewery.

High Street, late nineteenth century. The presence of a barn in the top picture is a sure sign that Cowley was still a rural village. In 1901 the population was recorded as 869. Beyond the barn is an ivy-covered building, shown more clearly in the lower photograph. This is the junction of the High Street and Fox Lane, although, as soon as Cowley station was opened, the latter became Station Road. Two policemen are standing in the roadway. The butcher's shop on the corner, with canopy over the entrance, survived until the junction was widened in 1958.

Cowley Lock from the south, *c.* 1905. A pair of Fellows, Morton and Clayton canal boats approach the lock. The coming of the canal enabled brick-making and gravel extraction to develop; later a coconut fibre factory was opened. The fibre was used to make ropes, mats and brushes.

Iver Lane from Shovel bridge, *c.* 1900. The Shovel public house, on the right, is a reminder that the canal was mostly dug by navvies using picks and shovels. On the opposite side of the road is a small beer house called the Harrow.

Cowley High Street, *c.* 1910. The canopy over the butcher's shop remains (see page 30), but beyond Station Road the old barn has been replaced by a house and a shop. The sign of the Fox public house is on the right.

Cowley station, October 1905. A train for West Drayton is approaching the platform. A request for a station here in the nineteenth century went unheeded, but GWR was spurred into action once its monopoly in the area was challenged by the Metropolitan Railway (see section 5). The station was opened in 1905.

Section Four

HILLINGDON VILLAGE IN ABOUT 1900

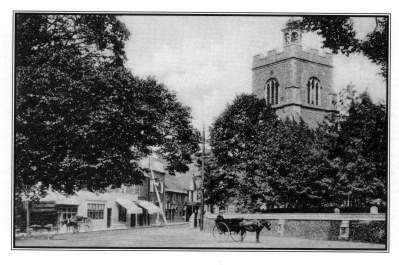

Hillingdon Village, c. 1905. The tower of the parish church of St John the Baptist rises above the churchyard trees. Some of the village shops are on the left.

St John's Church, 1898. On the extreme right is the Vine Inn, offering accommodation for travellers and cyclists and good stabling for horses. The Red Lion Inn is just visible in the distance.

The Red Lion overshadowed by a massive oak tree, c. 1908. Some years later this mighty oak was severely cut back, an atrocity which prompted a nearby resident to hang a sign on the tree bearing the single word 'Ichabod', which translates as 'the glory has departed' and is taken from I Samuel, chapter 4, verse 21.

William and Ruth Buttrum with their eleven children, 1905. The family came to Hillingdon from Suffolk in 1889. William ran a building business from premises near the Red Lion. (It is now an undertaker's.) He was also a noted wood carver, and some of his work survives in St John's Church. The children are, back row, left to right: Edith, Ella, Evaline, Frederick. Middle row: Alfred, Margaret (on her mother's lap). Front row: Cyril, Miriam, Albert, Harold, Adeline.

Mr Buttrum's workmen preparing to set off on a day's outing to Marlow, 1908. They travelled in two horse-drawn vehicles. In the background on the left is the building now known as the Cottage Hotel.

Alex Mitchell's saddler's shop, *c.* 1900. Alex (1847–1905) stands at the door on the right. The business had been in his family for several generations. He was prominent in local affairs, being a member of the Parish Council and a charity trustee. The shop was demolished in the 1930s.

The players, committee and officials, Hillingdon FC, *c.* 1898. Home games were played on Coney Green. Two players are wearing shin guards buckled over their socks, but the metal buckles were dangerous to other players and shin guards disappeared inside the socks.

An open-topped electric car of the London United Tramways passes the Red Lion on its way to Shepherds Bush, *c.* 1910. 'The electric car has enlivened the place', claimed a writer about this time. The landlord, W. Hicks, arms akimbo at the door, offered 'good accommodation for cyclists'; the emblem of the Cyclists Touring Club is visible below the lantern. In May 1903 the previous licensee, Ann Ashton, died in an upstairs room. She weighed twenty stone and it was virtually impossible to get her body down the narrow stairs. It was therefore passed out of the bay window on to the roof of a hearse strategically placed below.

The Cedar House, *c.* 1904. An Elizabethan mansion with Victorian additions, it takes its name from a mighty 53 ft high cedar tree. The tree was one of the first to be grown in this country and had been planted by a celebrated botanist, Samuel Reynardson, who lived here from 1678 to 1721. The tree on the left, which still survives, is probably a seedling from its illustrious ancestor. The building is now office accommodation.

The manor house at the top of Hillingdon Hill, north side. Strictly speaking it was not a manor house at all, having been built by a gentleman called Thomas Heming in about 1800. In the early 1930s it was demolished as part of a road-widening scheme, but nevertheless gave its name to Manor Parade, a row of shops with a sub-post office built nearby. The gardens and grounds of the estate were developed in the 1930s by builder R.T. Warren as The Rise estate.

LONDON REACHES OUT, 1904–7

GWR saddle-tank locomotive pulling five carriages towards Cowley station, c. 1910. In the cutting, beside Cleveland Road, may be seen the original Brunel-type permanent way on the left. In the distance are some of the greenhouses of the Lowe and Shawyer nurseries. From 1856 until 1904 this branch line from West Drayton was the only railway that the town had.

Metropolitan Railway building, *c.* 1904. In 1899 the Metropolitan Railway, which had reached Harrow-on-the Hill in 1880, obtained powers to build a branch line to Uxbridge. Work began in 1901, and by early 1904 the terminus station was ready (top picture). In the distance can be seen the Park Road bridge and some houses in Montague Road. (The site is today occupied by Sainsbury's supermarket.) The lower picture shows the layout of the goods yard and sidings looking towards York Road and Belmont Road. The station building was identical with that at Ruislip. Piccadilly line trains first came through to Uxbridge in 1933.

Official opening of Metropolitan branch line, 30 June 1904. Metropolitan locomotive No. 1, suitably decorated for the occasion, arrives at the Uxbridge platform. Some local residents were invited to travel on the train, and lunch was provided in a large marquee set up in the station yard. In a welcoming speech the local MP, Sir Frederick Dixon-Hartland, said that the Metropolitan Railway had 'rescued Uxbridge from decay'. This locomotive is still in working order and may be seen at the Buckinghamshire Railway Centre, a preserved railway at Quainton Road station.

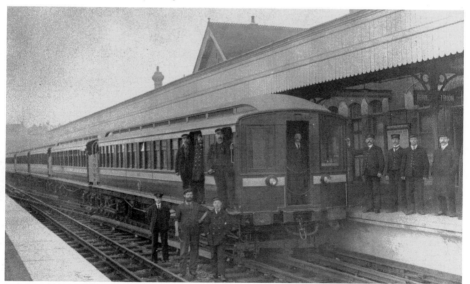

Trial of the first electric train, 22 November 1904. Regular steam services from Baker Street had begun on 4 July 1904. The line had been laid for steam or electric traction but the electric stock was not ready, and steam locomotives were used. From 1 January 1905 electric trains took over the Uxbridge service.

Tram lines being laid, Uxbridge High Street, January 1904. The London United Tramways, which had reached Southall in 1901, now obtained powers to extend their service through to Uxbridge. The terminus was near the junction of the High Street and Harefield Road. The house on the extreme left is now a McDonald's restaurant.

The first tramcar in Uxbridge, 31 May 1904. Tramcar No. 202 made its way into Uxbridge with a Board of Trade inspector, company directors and other local dignitaries on board. Crowds gathered, children were released from school to witness the occasion, and a celebratory lunch was held at the George Inn. The inspector gave authority for a public service to begin the following day.

Uxbridge tram terminus, soon after the service began, 1904. LUT route 7, Uxbridge to Shepherds Bush, ended here although some trams ran right through to Hammersmith. The fare from Uxbridge to Shepherds Bush was 5d. An enterprising gentleman called Dimsby immediately commenced a service of horse wagonettes linking the tram route with Denham village; one of his vehicles may well be standing on the left. It waits outside the Falcon Inn, which is today the Nonna Rosa restaurant. The Falcon moved to the larger building next door in 1924, and was re-named the Continental in 1984. Uxbridge people saw the coming of the trams as a further way of putting the town 'on the map'.

Uxbridge tram terminus, *c.* 1905. The Falcon is now stressing its dinners and teas, while, on the extreme right, the Terminus Tea Rooms are advertising too. By all accounts large numbers of people did travel to Uxbridge at weekends and holidays, and such places did a roaring trade. 'The place has been likened to Pandemonium,' said one contemporary writer.

A tram heading for Shepherds Bush near the junction of the High Street and Vine Street, *c.* 1905. This section of the main road was then known as 'St Andrew's'. On the left the canopy of Fletcher's the butchers straddles the pavement.

Uxbridge High Street station, *c.* 1910. In 1906 a new main line railway, initially known as the Acton and High Wycombe Railway, opened to the north. The Great Western Railway, which shared the route with the Great Central, built a branch line southwards to Uxbridge High Street station. It was roughly opposite the Treaty House, and was opened in May 1907.

Flight of stairs leading up to the platform, Uxbridge High Street station. The new station was built on an embankment and thus needed the stairs. Uxbridge, a town of moderate size, now had three railway stations – and all were termini. People began to speak of the town having an 'end-of-the-line' look. The intention of the GWR was to link their two branch lines, but the scheme was abandoned in 1913.

Uxbridge High Street station, probably in the late 1920s. A bridge was actually built over the High Street in 1907, but then the work came to an abrupt stop. The embankment beyond was never built, and the bridge was removed in May 1922. The Uxbridge High Street branch line never proved to be a financial success.

The GWR also offered road services, and here is one of their splendid charabancs outside St Margaret's Church, 1905. This was the start of a day's outing for the town's publicans. Note the chock behind the back wheel.

EDWARDIAN

UXBRIDGE

Windsor Street, 1902. Local people are putting up decorations in readiness to celebrate the
coronation of King Edward VII.

Hillingdon Road at the junction of The Greenway. Pleasant Place, the cottages on the left, still remain today. The Green Man public house on the opposite corner closed for alterations in the spring of 1995 and re-opened as a fish and chip restaurant.

The western end of The Greenway, looking towards Cowley Road, c. 1910. With many fairly large houses and a pleasant tree-lined route, the district had become quite an upper-class suburb of Uxbridge.

Rockingham Bridge, looking north, *c*. 1910. This was a favourite watering place for horses on Fray's river. Beyond the field on the left (later the Fassnidge Recreation Ground) are the buildings of Osborne, Stevens timber yard. On the extreme right is Rockingham Hall (see page 77) in the Lynch.

Fray's river, just off Cowley Road, *c*. 1910. Rabbs Mill chimney can be seen on the extreme left, and the houses of Bridge Road form the background. The iron bridge was replaced in 1993. Whitehall School opened near here in 1911.

The old Uxbridge almshouses, c. 1905. They were built in 1845 to replace an even earlier group of almshouses, built in 1728, a short distance away. In 1906 the newly formed Uxbridge United Charities decided to replace them. On the extreme right, complete with oriel window and flag-pole, is the headquarters of the Uxbridge Volunteer Fire Brigade.

The new almshouses, off New Windsor Street, March 1907. The charity trustees had asked a local architect, W.L. Eves, to design these buildings and the first occupants moved in early in 1907. The building survives, with some alteration, as Woodbridge House.

Uxbridge's first purpose-built post office. The old almshouses were demolished and the site cleared in September 1908 to build the new post office. The building was ready in December 1909. Enlarged in the early 1920s, and again in 1932, it was finally vacated by the Royal Mail in June 1990. It has since been converted into offices.

St Margaret's Hall, Belmont Road, 1908. The site had been acquired with money donated by a Miss Caroline Trevor, and she laid the foundation stone. Built as a parish hall, it was opened in May 1908. As with the new almshouses, the architect was W.L. Eves. It survived until March 1986. The Allied Irish Bank occupies the site today.

Uxbridge police station, Windsor Street. The Metropolitan Police area was extended to include the Uxbridge district in 1838, but the first police station was in Kingston Lane, Hillingdon. The building shown here replaced it in 1871, and by the time it closed in 1988 was the oldest purpose-built station in the Metropolitan area.

Uxbridge police in the yard of the Windsor Street premises, 1900. Inspector Brownscombe holds his ceremonial sword and is flanked by two station sergeants, each with four stripes on his arms. At this period the first floor of the building consisted of living accommodation for the inspector and his family, and for a few unmarried policemen.

The St Andrew's end of Uxbridge High Street, *c.* 1910. The signpost at the junction of Park Road is just visible in the distance. On the extreme left are Pool's dairy and the premises of Young, Son and Marlow, scale makers. The trees formed the boundary of the Park Lodge estate. The building on the right, with the small turret, is the head office of Fassnidge & Son, builders and contractors, a firm established in the late eighteenth century. They were the builders of St Andrew's Church, and one cannot help wondering if they used the surplus materials from that project to enhance their own headquarters.

Funeral of Benjamin Thomas Gales, 30 September 1908. It must be the most imposing funeral ever seen in the town's history. Mr Gales, an estate agent, had been deeply involved in the life of Uxbridge and for over thirty years had been chief officer of the Fire Brigade. The top picture shows the coffin (left), decorated with floral tributes, on the old manual fire engine outside his home, 75 High Street. Tickets were issued for the funeral service in St Margaret's Church. The long procession (below) then proceeded to the Uxbridge cemetery in Kingston Lane. With representatives from over thirty fire brigades present, all in full uniform, and a large parade of Oddfellows, the procession was about 400 yards long. Shops closed, and the whole town came to a standstill.

'Dick Turpin's Cottage, Uxbridge'. The title on this postcard is somewhat misleading as the famous highwayman never came anywhere near the town. Few notable events have taken place in Uxbridge, so people have been inventing its history for years. This early eighteenth-century cottage, latterly 118 Harefield Road, was also known as Marlin's Cottage. The Marlin family were involved with horses as farriers and veterinary surgeons, for several generations, and this doubtless fuelled the Turpin legend. J. Campden, the last owner, died in 1970. Shortly afterwards the cottage was demolished, and replaced by a modern house.

Harefield Road, *c.* 1910. The houses on the right still remain and form an attractive group. Until 1866 Harefield Road was known as Page's Lane, and was a rural, tree-lined route. This old name has been recently revived in a new housing development nearby.

Cowley Mill Road, *c.* 1910. Parked on end at the roadside is a two-wheeled builder's hand-cart. Also on the left is the Black Prince beer house, which closed in January 1969. The canal bridge is in the distance. It was always known as Swan bridge, because there was a public house called the Swan on the west side.

Section Seven

TRADE &
INDUSTRY, 1900–14

The butcher's shop of Henry Joseph Kew, 45 Windsor Street, c. 1905. Mr Kew (left)
learned his trade in a family business at (confusingly) Kew, and opened this Uxbridge shop
in 1902. He imported mutton and lamb from Canterbury in New Zealand. Note the
punning slogan 'Q for quality' below the hanging carcases.

Cowley Mill, or Rabbs Mill, as rebuilt after the fire of 1898 (see page 17). Cowley Road is on the left. Another fire, in February 1928, brought milling to a close. A small part of the building survives today as the Hale Hamilton valve works.

Workers in one of the chrysanthemum houses, Lowe and Shawyer's nursery, c. 1912. This cut-flower nursery was founded by Joseph Lowe in 1864, and it specialised in growing roses and chrysanthemums for the London market. After 1897, when George Shawyer became his partner, the nursery, off Kingston Lane, expanded rapidly. By 1914 the area cultivated was 71 acres, and there were 300 employees.

Ada Staniford's newsagent's shop, 52 Windsor Street. Mrs Staniford also sold stationery and tobacco. The Staniford family, who came from the Woburn area of Bedfordshire, at first had a butcher's shop in the High Street. William Staniford bought this shop about 1910 and he and his wife later took a second similar shop in Cowley Road.

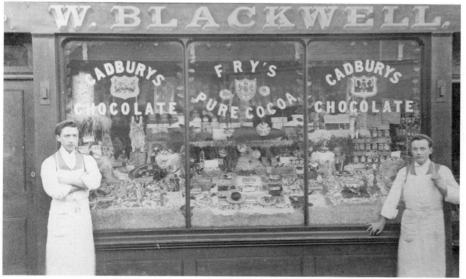

Blackwell's confectionery shop, 5 Windsor Street, c. 1906. James Joseph Blackwell (left) and his brother William Howard Blackwell stand outside the business founded there by their grandfather in about 1839. The shop was noted for its home-made biscuits, cakes, sweets, pickles and jams. This is a Christmas display, probably in 1906 when James and William had just taken over the business from their father.

Timber yards, Osborne, Stevens & Co., Grand Junction Canal, *c.* 1900. The view is from the Swan and Bottle bridge. The firm was founded by the Osborne family in 1760 and received an enormous boost with the arrival of the canal. The company then dealt in timber, slate and coal, all brought from the river Thames. Thomas Osborne entered into partnership with Henry Stevens in about 1850.

Swing bridge, Osborne, Stevens timber yards, *c.* 1900. The bridge swung over an L-shaped arm of the canal leading to Fountain's Mill. By this time dealing in slate and coal had ceased, and timber was being imported from north Germany and Scandinavia via the London docks.

Procter's carriage-building works, 42 New Windsor Street, c. 1905. Edward Procter initially worked at Dobell's flour mill maintaining their horse-drawn vehicles. He left to launch his own business. With the advent of the motor car the firm became Procter's Motors, and it moved to premises in Uxbridge High Street. In 1959 Proctor's was taken over by Locomotors Limited, which ceased trading in 1970.

The premises of Joseph Nicholls, pork butcher and poulterer, 3 New Windsor Street, January 1908. The business had been established by his father, George Nicholls, in the High Street in about 1830, but when New Windsor Street was opened up in the 1840s Joseph moved there. It was acknowledged that his pork sausages surpassed all others in the district for flavour. He died in 1905, and the shop passed to his sons.

Bradfield's, the corn, flour and seed merchants, 28 High Street. Charles Bradfield founded the firm in 1877 and it became one of the leading shops in the town. He died in 1891 and his widow Mary Elizabeth continued it thereafter. The Midland Bank took over these premises in 1921 and the upper part of the building is still recognisable today.

Cosy Tea Rooms, 2 Windsor Street, 1910. Proprietor Sam Mutters had spent the early part of his life touring as 'little Sam Waller', juggler, clown and pantomimist, and described himself as 'Britain's premier nose-balancer'. There is a limit to what any one nose can take, and Sam, and his wife Lily (seen here), retired to Uxbridge to run this café and lodging-house. The building was demolished in 1928. Much-needed public lavatories were erected on the site. Everyone was relieved.

The western end of the High Street, 1905. On the extreme left is Fountain's Mill; part of this building survives today. On the right is a beer house called the Audrey Arms, which was rented in the 1880s as a weekend cottage by the famous actress Ellen Terry (1848–1928). The building was dismantled just prior to the Second World War, the intention being to erect it elsewhere, but when the war was over much of the material had 'disappeared'.

The hardware and ironmongery shop of Kirby Bros., 154 High Street. The business was founded by the brothers Frank and Bob Kirby in 1913. After the First World War they became builders' merchants too, and by the 1930s the firm, with over 100 employees, was serving a wide area.

John Ward, carpenter and builder, (seated in the centre) with his workmen outside their premises in Wellington Road, *c.* 1902. Sitting in front are his grandchildren. The photograph may well have been taken to mark the coronation of King Edward VII in August of that year.

Laying electricity cables, *c.* 1900. The Uxbridge Electricity Supply Company was formed in 1899 and a generating station was built in Waterloo Road next to the canal. The first public supply of electricity in the Uxbridge area was made on 1 May 1902.

Lucy & Birch, 45 High Street. The origins of the firm lay in the eighteenth century, but in Victorian times they were booksellers and stationers with a printing department at the rear of the premises. To this was added a subscription library, and by this time they had developed a sideline in sports equipment as well. The business closed in 1930.

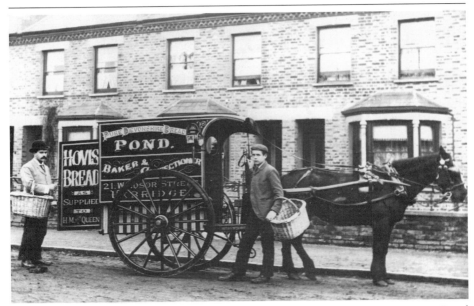

Lewis Pond and his son James on their baker's round, Uxbridge, *c.* 1900. Mr Pond acquired the bakery business at 21 Windsor Street in 1891, and handed it on to James in 1920. The family sold the business in about 1970.

Lipton's, 25 High Street, 1917. The manager, Mr Crosby, stands behind his staff. Lipton's opened in 1908, but their application to sell intoxicating liquor caused an uproar the following year. It was calculated that Uxbridge already had seventy-three licensed premises – twice as many in proportion to its population as the rest of England.

The premises of Alfred Pond, dyer and cleaner, 78 St Andrew's. Young Sid Pond is shown here outside his father's shop which was later re-numbered 208 High Street. The Ponds' slogan was 'We dye to live'. The shop was gutted by fire in August 1909, but was refurbished. Alfred Pond died in 1918.

T.P. Edwards, greengrocer and fishmonger, 51 Windsor Street, c. 1903. The proprietor is in the doorway, hands behind his back. The smaller of the two boys on the right is his son, who eventually took over from his father.

Telephone men outside Uxbridge post office, 182 High Street, probably early in 1903. The service was launched in that year. Rather like BT and Mercury today, at this period the GPO was rivalled by the National Telephone Company, who had established their exchange in Vine Street in 1901. By the time the two merged, in 1912, there were 164 subscribers.

The Steel Barrel Company and its workers, 1905–10. The company was established in Uxbridge in 1897 by an engineer named Thomas Heaton. Shortly afterwards electric power became available, the business grew, and in 1905 a larger works on a 5-acre site off Rockingham Road was opened. The photograph above, taken at about that time, shows employees operating a machine which is shaping the steel. When the company started about twenty men were employed, but this number rapidly increased to about sixty by 1910. The group below includes Henry Eves, standing to the right with his hands on a colleague's shoulders.

Bert Burrows' funeral hearse, outside St Margaret's Hall, *c.* 1910. As a young man Bert spent some time working as a cowboy in Texas, but eventually returned to Uxbridge to help his father run the family business in George Yard. They were fly proprietors, carriers and undertakers. From 1907 to 1919 they supplied the horses for the Uxbridge fire engine. Bert, a member of the brigade, drove the appliance of course.

Gregory's yard, 53 High Street, 1912. Early Ford cars are for sale. Frederick Gregory had been a fruiterer, florist, greengrocer and bill poster before he entered the cycle and car trade. Gregory's Motors was founded in 1903. Mr Gregory was also town crier of Uxbridge.

E.R. Butler returning to his chauffeur-driven car, 1910. He was a traveller – what would now be called a sales rep – and has just collected an order from a shop in Englefield Green. The wholesale grocery firm of Alfred Button & Sons was based in a depot off Belmont Road next to the Metropolitan Railway station. By 1910 they were serving a wide area.

Foden steam lorry, Button's depot, c. 1907. Grocery orders were processed at Button's depot and then sent out to local stores. At first this was done using horse-drawn wagons, but in 1907 the company purchased this splendid steam lorry for delivery runs. Its maximum speed was 5 mph. Their first petrol-driven vehicles came into use in 1912.

Warren Farm, northern end of Harefield Road, 1913. Although the district was rapidly changing from a country area into a London suburb, farms like this survived well into the twentieth century. This 46-acre farm formed part of the Harefield Place estate, and took its name from an enormous rabbit warren nearby where, at one time, hundreds of rabbits existed in the wild. In 1810 the warren was said to be the only substantial one left in the county of Middlesex, and even today there is a Warren Road to serve as a reminder.

EDWARDIAN SPORT
& LEISURE

Uxbridge Bowls Club, c. 1913. The club was formed in that year on a corner of the
Uxbridge Cricket Club ground.

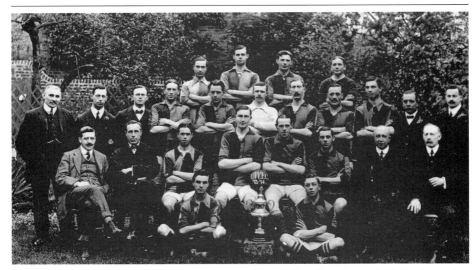

Uxbridge Wednesday FC, winners of the Windsor Wednesday Cup, 1914. Early closing day in Uxbridge was Wednesday, and so this side was made up of young men who worked in local shops and who could not turn out on a Saturday afternoon.

Olympic marathon runners, St John's Road, Uxbridge Moor, 1908. That year the Olympic Games were held in London at the White City stadium. The marathon race was started in the grounds of Windsor Castle and the runners passed through Uxbridge on their way to the stadium. Unfortunately the quality of the photograph leaves a lot to be desired.

Olympic marathon runners between Uxbridge and Ickenham, 1908. In front is Johnny Hayes, No. 26, of the USA, who was the eventual winner. The event is best remembered because the Italian, P. Dorando, entered the stadium first, collapsed within a few yards of the finish, was carried over the line by enthusiastic supporters, and was inevitably disqualified.

Start of a round-the-town race for boys outside the George Inn, High Street, 26 August 1908. The Olympic marathon, held a few weeks earlier, seems to have inspired local people to organise this race as part of the annual Sports Day held on August bank holiday at Uxbridge cricket field.

Uxbridge Rovers Angling Society, c. 1900. The society was formed in 1884, but fishing in local rivers had been going on for centuries before that. Eels from the clear waters of the river Colne were regarded as a local delicacy.

Huntsmoor Weir, Cowley, c. 1912. Mr Weston (right), proprietor of a tobacconist's shop in Windsor Street, is fishing for trout assisted by Mr Bunn, the water bailiff, who probably controlled the fishing rights here.

The 1st Uxbridge Scout Troop, 1918. It was founded in 1908 by six teenage lads who were inspired by Baden-Powell's book *Scouting For Boys*. Here some of the troop proudly display the Stilwell Shield, a district trophy awarded for camping skills. It is wartime, and Jessie Finch has more than ably taken over the role of 'scoutmaster'.

The first 'picture palace' in Uxbridge, Rockingham Hall in the Lynch, *c.* 1910. It opened in the August of that year and admission was *3d* or *6d*. There were two shows every evening, at 7 p.m. and 9 p.m., and two matinees every Saturday afternoon. So many people wanted to see these early, silent, black-and-white movies that the cinema was soon superseded by a larger one in Vine Street, the Uxbridge Electric Empire (see page 108).

Uxbridge Show, 1914. Organised by the Uxbridge and District Horticultural Society, the first show was held in 1909. It was planned as a flower and horticultural show, and proved so successful that it became an annual event and included a wider range of activities. Seen here is a line of competitors for the best turned-out tradesman's vehicle. They are outside the gate of Park Lodge, a large house in Park Road, about half a mile from Uxbridge Common showground. In 1966 the event was re-named the Hillingdon Show, and three years later became a two-day event. Since 1986 it has been known as the Middlesex Show.

EDUCATION IN THE EARLY TWENTIETH CENTURY

A class at Hillingdon Girls School, Royal Lane, c. 1905. The girls are dressed in pinafores and wearing laced or buttoned boots. The school closed in 1928 and the building was converted to become the parish hall.

Belmont Road Girls School, *c.* 1914. The school was established by a charity in 1816, and was known as the School of Industry for Girls. (In those days 'industry' meant 'useful work'.) In 1909 the school had been taken over by the Middlesex County Council and re-named.

Belmont Road Girls School, *c.* 1914. This time the class is lined up in the playground. In the background on the right is St Margaret's Hall. In the roadway stands a council dust cart pulled by a white horse.

Whitehall School, Cowley Road, *c.* 1914. This school was opened by the county in October 1911, and replaced an earlier and smaller school in New Windsor Street. 'Sit up straight with your hands behind your backs' seems to have been the order given to these girls and boys.

St John's Church of England School, Uxbridge Moor, *c.* 1900. The school was founded in 1843, a few years after the creation of the parish. On the right is Robert Sargeant, headmaster from 1869 to 1911 – a remarkable forty-two years.

St Margaret's School in the Lynch, 1916. This school, for boys and girls, opened in 1864 and survived until 1928. On the right is Guy Lawrence, who was headmaster from 1915 until the closure.

A class of budding violinists at Cowley Road Boys School, c. 1905. Like the Belmont Road Girls School, it was founded as a charity school and later taken over by the Middlesex Education Committee. It too closed in 1928, when a major re-organisation of education took place in the Uxbridge area. Seated on the left is headmaster Edward Cole, the subject of a 'scurrilous' rhyme: 'Mr Cole is a very good man/ He goes to church on Sunday/ To ask the Lord to give him strength/ To whack the boys on Monday'.

The new Uxbridge County School, The Greenway. The 1902 Education Act had given County Councils the powers to provide secondary education, and Middlesex duly responded: this school opened in September 1907. The school was designed for 150 pupils, most of whom were expected to pay fees. On the left of the photograph is a two-storey block with specially equipped rooms for cookery (for girls) and manual training (for boys).

Open-air art class, Uxbridge County School, *c.* 1910. The teacher, Mr Watson, watches over the pupils. The girls' uniform was a blouse and ankle-length skirt; the ribbon on their straw hats bore the Middlesex coat-of-arms. For the boys green blazers and caps were the rule.

Cookery teacher, Janie Morrison, Uxbridge County School. The provision of well-equipped rooms for cookery, manual training and science at the school was regarded as a great advance at the time. Miss Morrison came from Glasgow and was the first cookery teacher employed. As well as teaching, her duties included managing lunch in the cookery room for pupils living some distance from the school. Her annual salary was £80.

Section Ten

THE FIRST WORLD WAR & ITS AFTERMATH

Hillingdon House and Park, 1913. Note the splendid orangery in the distance. Here the river Pinn has been widened into a lake.

Hillingdon House, 1914. This picture comes from a sales brochure. The Cox family, London bankers, were selling the extensive estate, including this splendid 26-bedroom mansion built in 1845. In 1915 HM Government permanently took over the house and park.

In 1915 Hillingdon House became a convalescent home for Canadian soldiers sent back from the battlefields of France and Belgium; some are seen here relaxing outside. A detachment of the Royal Army Medical Corps looked after them. In 1917 the Royal Flying Corps (RFC) took over the estate.

Armament and Gunnery School of the RFC, 1917. Previously at Perivale, it was transferred to Uxbridge, and here some of the trainee air gunners practise on the ranges. Soon the noise of 2,500 men firing Vickers and Lewis machine-guns reverberated over Uxbridge.

King George V visiting Uxbridge camp, 2 May 1918. On 1 April the Royal Flying Corps had been re-named the Royal Air Force. Here the king inspects members of the Women's Air Force Auxiliary (WAFA) outside Hillingdon House. Their none-too-flattering greatcoats led them to be nicknamed 'the penguins'.

On his tour of RAF Uxbridge the king was given a demonstration of synchronisation, since in those days the air gunners fired through the revolving blades of the propeller. Using the equipment shown above, it was proved to the royal visitor that bullet holes through a disc of tin were in positions that indicated the propeller would not be hit.

Women of the Air Force Auxiliary, c. 1918. At this period the duties of the WAFA appear to have been almost entirely domestic: cooking, cleaning and acting as waitresses in the Officers' Mess. The gentleman in the centre is Lieutenant Hopkins, who bore the grand title of Messing Officer.

Able seaman Cyril Buttrum (see page 35) marries Kate Johnson, January 1916. The ceremony took place in Hillingdon parish church, and the wedding party is grouped outside the bridegroom's home. A few weeks later Cyril was drowned at the Battle of Jutland. Kate died in 1954, having never re-married. The First World War brought many such tragedies.

Lads from Uxbridge County School, Richardson's Farm, Cowley. They have been picking fruit to aid the war effort. Girls from the school also did farm work, and even the school garden was transformed into a vegetable patch. The group includes George Yonge (left) and Will Stears (front row, centre).

Corps of Drums, RAF Central Band, 1924. In 1920 Uxbridge became the home of the RAF Central Band, and its presence has brought prestige to the town ever since. The Corps of Drums frequently performed at the British Empire Exhibition at Wembley in 1924 and 1925.

Decorated wagon, Uxbridge Peace Celebrations, 19 July 1919. Girls from St Andrew's School are on board. The planned events lasted from 8 a.m. until midnight, and included a procession headed by the Uxbridge and Hillingdon Band.

Peace Day procession, 19 July 1919. This decorated vehicle was prepared by Randall's Stores of Vine Street (see page 14). The brothers Philip and William Randall moved from High Wycombe to Uxbridge in 1891 to establish their furnishing store. Over a century later Randall's stores is still in Vine Street, and run by Philip's great-grandson John.

The war memorial at the junction of Park Road and the High Street. It was unveiled by the dowager Lady Hillingdon on 9 November 1924. On the right is an entrance to RAF Uxbridge, with replica bombs on the gate piers. A further inscription was added to the memorial after the Second World War. (In 1972, prior to the construction of the St Andrew's roundabout, the memorial was moved to the former burial ground at the southern end of Windsor Street.)

Armistice Day, c. 1935. The annual observance of Armistice Day on 11 November, and the impressive two-minute silence at 11 a.m., became features of life after the First World War. The veterans shown here are about to take part in an armistice parade. They are grouped outside Uxbridge High Street station, with its long staircase leading to the elevated platform.

UXBRIDGE IN THE 1920s

Harefield Road, c. 1920. On the extreme left is the beginning of a footpath leading to Fray's Farm and Denham. On the right beyond the houses is the narrow entrance to Gravel Hill.

The Bell Punch Company's factory, 1920s. The canal bridge and Dolphin Inn are in the lower left-hand corner. The company was formed in London in 1878 to manufacture hand-operated ticket punches and tickets for London trams. The first bell punch was made in about 1890. The company moved to the Uxbridge site in 1919.

Some of the 400 workers at the Bell Punch factory, c. 1920. The bell punch and pre-printed tickets were supplied to many countries, and to these were added automatic ticket-machines for cinemas. In 1929, after talks with the Race Course Betting Control Board, a totalisator machine was developed that became standard in this country and the USA.

The Manipulation of
the Z.N. Bell Punch

The cover of a handbook issued by the company to London Transport employees to explain the use of a bell punch. The conductor inserted a coloured and numbered ticket, marked with the fare, into a slot at the top of the machine. He pressed a lever at the bottom, a bell rang, a hole was punched in the ticket, and the clipping fell into a compartment inside. Meanwhile a numerator registered the number of times the lever was depressed. All these were safeguards to ensure that neither the passenger nor the bus company was defrauded. London Transport ceased to use the bell punch about 1950.

Park Road, *c.* 1925. The sub-post office and the Gardeners Arms are on the left. On the right is the narrow entrance to Honeycroft Hill, which until 1935 was known as Ickenham Road.

A one-man operated Dennis Dart bus, Uxbridge terminus, *c.* 1930. The building behind the bus is the New Inn, Windsor Street. The first buses were seen in Uxbridge in 1921, when the London General Omnibus Company commenced services to Hounslow and High Wycombe. A garage was built on the Oxford Road at Denham in 1922.

The northern part of the Fassnidge Recreation Ground, late 1920s. Osborne, Stevens timber yard is on the left, and Sedgwick's Brewery is behind the trees. Kate Fassnidge gave 6 acres of land to the people of Uxbridge in memory of her husband, and this memorial park was opened in October 1926. A bandstand, paddling pool, swings and tennis courts were included in the scheme.

Fassnidge Bowls Club, c. 1928. In part of the recreation ground a bowling green was prepared, and there the club came into being in 1928. Mrs Fassnidge was elected president. She is seen here in her wheelchair with some of the members. She died in 1950 and bequeathed her own house and garden to the townspeople. To her left is Walter G. Pomeroy JP, who was a local councillor for twenty-six years, and chairman of the council throughout the Second World War.

In 1927 the people of Uxbridge in Massachusetts celebrated the bicentenary of the foundation of their town. Mr and Mrs Charles King (right) were sent to the USA as delegates representing Uxbridge, England, and are seen here on their departure from Vine Street station. Mr King was joint managing director of the local printing and newspaper firm of King & Hutchings Ltd. James Cochrane, chairman of Uxbridge Council, holds an illuminated address to be presented in America. (There is an Uxbridge in Ontario, Canada and another very small settlement called Uxbridge in Tasmania.)

Part of the Lowe and Shawyer cut-flower nurseries, 1929. Cleveland Road and the GWR branch line run across the centre of the photograph, with The Greenway bridge on the right. At about this time the nursery took the decision to concentrate more on carnations and, beyond the railway, on the left, work is proceeding on the construction of twenty-two new greenhouses for this purpose. Rose growing ceased shortly after this.

Section Twelve

COWLEY IN THE 1930s

Cowley High Street, 1938. Buildings belonging to Maygoods Farm are on the left. On the right are some of the council houses in Maygoods View.

Another section of the winding High Street, 1938. On the right are some newly built shops in Dellfield Parade. On the left is the garage of 'Brassy' Bryant. The rider of the motor-cycle combination may well be 'Brassy' himself.

A third section of the High Street, looking south, 1938. The recreation ground is beyond the iron railings on the right. On the left a board advertises new houses in Dellfield Crescent at £645.

Section Thirteen

HILLINGDON IN THE 1930s

Royal Lane, Hillingdon, 1930. The building in the centre is called The Cottage. Today the ambulance station for Hillingdon Hospital occupies this spot, but at this period it was still a haven of rural tranquillity.

Looking up the hill towards St John's Church, Hillingdon village, 1934. The Red Lion is on the right. On the left are shops and cottages, which are about to be demolished in connection with a road widening scheme. Much of the character of the village was lost through this change.

Vine Lane, 1934. It still has the appearance of a country lane. About half a mile further on were two large houses. Hillingdon House, on the left, had become RAF Uxbridge. Hillingdon Court, on the right, formerly the home of Lord Hillingdon, had become a convent school.

Bishopshalt School. To the south of Hillingdon village lay a red-brick house built in 1858 by a London builder, John Jackson. Earlier houses on the site had belonged to the Bishops of Worcester, hence, presumably, the name Bishopshalt. In 1925 Middlesex County Council bought the estate and the house was altered and enlarged to provide a new home for Uxbridge County School (see page 83). In 1930 the school was re-named Bishopshalt School.

New shops and Vine Inn, Hillingdon village, 1936. On the ground behind the lamp post are the last vestiges of the old shops and cottages shown opposite. In front of the new shops is a service road, which was later converted into part of a dual carriageway.

Hillingdon Hill, mid-1930s. At this time the road was made into a dual carriageway. The old thoroughfare, on the left, became the 'down' route, although trams were still coming up! On the right R.T. Warren was building houses on The Rise estate.

A girls' cookery class, Hillingdon Primary School, 1936. To the right stands David Aubrey, headmaster from 1918 to 1948.

Long Lane, *c.* 1930. The land on both sides belonged to Lord Hillingdon, and therefore there was little development until his estate was sold in 1919. After that things happened quickly, and between the First and Second World Wars the whole area of North Hillingdon became a vast housing estate, with shops, schools and churches.

New shops, North Hillingdon, 1935. At the end of the shops Long Lane was crossed by the new Western Avenue, and already the section to London was open. The extension from Long Lane to Park Road, Uxbridge, was ready in 1937.

Steam roller laying a road on part of the Oak Farm estate, *c.* 1933. The semi-detached houses in the background, built by Webster & Co., are being offered at £740.

Oak Farm, off Long Lane, *c.* 1925. Here is a last glimpse of the farm before it was engulfed by houses. The 263-acre farm was bought from Lord Hillingdon by Alfred Smith, a market gardener from Feltham. After Smith's death in 1927 the land was sold for housing. These unknown individuals appear to be finishing a milk round.

UXBRIDGE IN THE
1930s

Uxbridge war memorial, southern end of Park Road (see page 92). On the left is the

Central Hall, opened by the Methodist church in 1930.

The Electric Empire Cinema, Vine Street, pictured just after its closure. It opened in 1910, and held 500 people. However, the larger Savoy and Regal cinemas made it obsolete and it closed in 1932.

The same building converted to become Uxbridge Fire Station, 1933. It remained the headquarters of the local fire service until 1964, and was then altered to become a youth workshop. It was demolished in August 1984.

The Regal cinema. It opened on Boxing Day 1931. Designed by architect E. Norman Bailey, it had 1,700 seats and no gallery. A car park at the rear held 300 cars. In its first year 750,000 people paid for admission.

The detached console of the Compton organ, Regal cinema. During the intervals between films, the console would rise centre stage and organ music would fill the auditorium.

Uxbridge High Street, early 1930s. Vehicles parked at the kerb made traffic impossibly congested. Here the breakdown of a small car has halted all movement in both directions. It was expected that the Western Avenue would prove to be a much-needed by-pass. The Savoy cinema is on the left of the picture.

First trolleybus in Uxbridge, on a trial run, 9 November 1936. It is seen here outside the Falcon Inn. Route 607, from Shepherds Bush to Uxbridge, replaced the old trams six days later. Trolleybuses ran until November 1960.

The Swan and Bottle public house, *c.* 1935. The rustic seats invited cyclists and motorists to pause on their journeys. As an added attraction the landlord had a cage of small monkeys in the yard, which certainly appealed to children.

The main street of Denham, 1930. Three miles north-west of Uxbridge lay this picturesque Buckinghamshire village and here there is as yet no sign of twentieth-century intervention. The mighty trees in the churchyard dominate the background. In February 1935 an estate to the north of the village was purchased by London Films, and the construction of film studios followed speedily.

Uxbridge Vine Street station, *c.* 1935. The over-all roof (see page 14) has been replaced by a canopy roof over the platform.

Uxbridge Cricket Club, 1933. The club had its origins in the eighteenth century. The ground at the end of Cricketfield Road was its home from 1858 until 1970. Back row, left to right: F. Read, J. Austin (umpire), M. Gibbs, T. Lawford, J. Pomeroy, T. Male, J. Richardson. Middle row: J. Coles (treasurer), G. Taylor, C. Stevens (president), S. Ward (captain and honorary secretary), W.L. Eves (vice-president; he was also a noted local architect – see pages 50, 51 and 117). Front row: E. Brown, H. Marks, F. Alford.

Vine Street, *c.* 1934 The side wall of the Savoy cinema is on the left. The narrow exit into the High Street is about to be widened by the demolition of the doctors' surgery on the right. Through the gap can be seen the Uxbridge branch of the National Provincial Bank, opened in December 1932 at 174 High Street.

Belmont Road. This was also widened at its High Street end. On the right can be seen the White Horse public house and Barclays Bank. The buildings opposite were cleared in 1936, including the Kirby Bros. showroom (see page 63). On the extreme left is Lion Yard, and the sign of F.W. Cross, farrier.

Shops on the south side of Vine Street, 1933. Beyond the narrow entrance to Cricketfield Road is Randall's Stores, whose premises were rebuilt in the late 1930s. The large block on the right looks rather dilapidated, but this is mainly owing to the poor condition of the canopy over the pavement.

Lower end of Vine Street, c. 1937. The cottages of Vine Street Terrace are on the right. On the left are the railings round the old burial ground, which were removed in 1938 to improve the field of vision of motorists at the junction of Vine Street, Windsor Street and Cowley Road.

The Silver Jubilee of King George V in May 1935 was celebrated with gusto by people in the Uxbridge area. As their contribution to a procession round the town, the members of the Uxbridge Fire Brigade have decorated an old horse-drawn fire engine found on the Breakspear estate at Harefield. The Railway Arms is on the left; the fire station is on the right.

Coronation celebrations, 12 May 1937. The market house is suitably adorned in red, white and blue. As in 1935, a full day's programme was arranged. It ended in the late evening with a torchlight procession to Uxbridge Common, a mammoth bonfire and a fireworks display.

George Snoad outside his grocery store, 7 Vine Street, 1933. Those were still the days when grocers went to great pains to mount a fine display of their wares in the shop window. George Snoad's reward for displaying a Regal cinema board outside his shop was two free cinema tickets every Wednesday afternoon. He retired in 1937.

Some of the immaculate carnation houses at Lowe and Shawyer nursery, 1930s. On 25 April 1934 Queen Mary, accompanied by the young Princess Elizabeth, spent an hour touring the nursery. By 1938 there were 1,400 employees in the peak summer period, and well over 50 million blooms were sold that year.

Opening of Uxbridge Swimming Pool, 31 August 1935. Revd Luther Bouch, chairman of Uxbridge Council, delivers a speech at the ceremony. Prior to this, people either travelled miles to other municipal baths, or used a bathing area on the Fray's river just north of Fountains Mill. There was civic pride at this new achievement.

Uxbridge Swimming Pool. The pool was 220 ft long and had a café (left). Built in five months by G. Percy Trentham, to the designs of W.L. Eves, the pool cost £24,500. At the Olympic Games of 1948 RAF Uxbridge was the Olympic village, and many swimming competitors trained in these baths.

Bell Yard, just opposite the market house, off the High Street. This was one of the many yards and alleys that were developed in the nineteenth century; it had been a slum for a long time. Relief came in 1936 when the area was purchased by London Transport in order to erect a new terminus station.

Baker's Yard. The yard took its name from James Baker, who had a china shop by the High Street entrance at the beginning of the nineteenth century. The yard was a short distance away from Bell Yard, and it was also acquired as part of the station project. Soon the demolition of the cottages, shops and outbuildings followed.

High Street shops opposite the market house. These were demolished to make way for the curved forecourt of the new station. Most of the firms shown here took shops in the frontage of the new building.

Work on the new station, 1937. The buildings in the distance are in York Road. In 1933 Piccadilly line trains came through to Uxbridge for the first time, and the original Metropolitan station off Belmont Road became inadequate. The new terminus opened on 4 December 1938.

The Odeon, which opened in Uxbridge on 20 June 1938. It was the town's fourth cinema: the Savoy, Regal and RAF cinemas were the others. Designed by Andrew Mather and Keith Roberts, it cost £50,400 to build. There were 622 seats in the circle and a further 1,215 in the stalls below.

Wilmar Close, Uxbridge, 1939. These youngsters were not much concerned with the growing menace of Nazi Germany. Their main aim was to get a penny Snofrute from the Walls ice-cream man, who pedalled his tricycle daily from the firm's depot at Hillingdon Heath. The cheeky stripling wearing the vendor's hat is the author. The other children are, back row, left to right: Bobby Dell, Harold Newby, Ian Bray, Beryl Gorman, David Smith. Front row: Don Burton, Esther Newby, Rosalie Pearce.

Section Fifteen

A FEW NOTABLE CHARACTERS

Giles Hutson (1823–1904) spent his entire career
as a saddler and harness maker in Uxbridge High
Street. In 1884 he recorded his recollections of the
town in his boyhood at the peak of the era of the
stage-coach. They make fascinating reading.

James Bunce (1788–1865) was the blacksmith in Hillingdon village. Standing 6 ft 2 in tall, and weighing 23 stone in his prime, Bunce always wore knee breeches, buckled shoes and a broad-rimmed hat. When fire broke out at Hillingdon House in 1844, he is said to have carried a piano from the blazing house single-handed: 'The smith a mighty man was he,' to quote the words of an old song. He is shown here at the door of his cottage; during his 77 years, he never slept away from this property, in which he had been born. His forge was just across the road at the rear of the Red Lion inn.

George Case (1812–67) was known to everyone in Uxbridge as 'Nobby Casey'. He earned a living by doing simple jobs such as putting up the stalls in the market house or carrying soft water for local laundresses using a yoke and two buckets. Nobby was also able to supplement his income by using his remarkable and unfailing memory. Once he learned the date of a person's birth or wedding he never forgot it, and, on the anniversary of the event, would greet them in the street or at their home with his good wishes. These gestures usually brought him some reward – even occasionally half-a-crown.

Vernon Gaylard (1870–1945) (left) and his brother Hugh (1872–1946) were both outstanding footballers with Uxbridge FC. This portrait was probably taken in 1890 when they both played for the county of Middlesex as well. They were the sons of a High Street chemist, who combined that role with being postmaster of Uxbridge. Vernon eventually managed a chemist's shop. Hugh, or 'Du' as he was always known, played for Middlesex on over 50 occasions and also for QPR as a guest. His obituary in the local press stated that he was 'one of the best full-backs in the South of England'. He later became licensee of the Chiltern View Tavern.

Lord and Lady Hillingdon in the grounds of Hillingdon Court, *c.* 1918. The family fortune was based on a partnership in the private banking firm of Glyn, Mills, Currie & Co. in Lombard Street. Charles Mills (1792–1872) bought the extensive Hillingdon estate in about 1850, and built a new house called Hillingdon Court soon afterwards. His son Sir Charles Mills (1830–98) was created Baron Hillingdon in 1886 for political and public services. Here the second Lord Hillingdon (1855–1919) sits in a horse-drawn invalid carriage, with his wife, daughter of Baron Suffield, holding the reins. After Lord Hillingdon died in 1919 the estate was sold and the family moved away. Hillingdon Court is now an American Community School. The barony became extinct in 1982.

Joseph Lowe (1844–1929) (left) and George Shawyer (1864–1943) at Mr Lowe's home in Kingston Lane, Hillingdon, *c.* 1924. Joseph Lowe bought the Kingston Lane land in 1868, and his cut-flower nursery steadily expanded. A spell of ill-health in 1897 caused him to take into partnership a young Cranford man named George Eldred Shawyer, and the two men proved ideally suited. Under their leadership the Lowe and Shawyer nursery became one of the largest in the country, and by 1935 it extended to almost 200 acres. It was by far the greatest employer of labour in the Uxbridge area. Both Mr Lowe and Mr Shawyer were awarded the Victoria Medal of Honour, the highest award granted by the Royal Horticultural Society.

The actor Bernard Miles (1907–91) was born in New Road, Hillingdon Heath. His acting ability first became apparent at Uxbridge County School, where he was encouraged by drama teacher Cecilia Hill. The photograph shows Bernard as the hunchback king in the school production of Shakespeare's *Richard III* in 1926. 'He made the man live before us in all his pride of intellect, ruthlessness and cruelty,' wrote one critic. A career on stage, screen and television followed. One of his specialities was rustic monologues in a broad Buckinghamshire accent. His place in theatre history is assured by his founding of the Mermaid Theatre at Puddle Dock in 1959. As Lord Miles of Blackfriars he became a life peer in 1979.

Index

Acknowledgements

Bishopshalt School • Hilda Browne • Audrey Bunce • Sue Curley • Pat Finch
1st Uxbridge Scouts • John Fricker • Richard Gaylard • *Gazette* newspaper
Freda Gent • Peter Grace • Julian Jephcote • Betty Kingston • Rene Kitchen
Rene Marks • Sam Mutters • John Shepherd • Ruth Simpson
Ken Thompson • Barbara Townsend • Lilian Tugwell • Norah Wilkins
Ella Williams • Kay Woods